How to use this Booklet
Glance through quickly in the morning before work, at lunch and before bed. It will be on your mind 24/7 making you an expert PMP before and after the exam.

July 2020 Exam Updates
Exam content will not change but percentage weight of questions will increase to 42 percent and 8 percent in people and business domain respectively and process will decrease to 50 percent.

Mapping Domains to Project Processes

Domain	Percentage of Items on Test
I. People	42%
II. Process	50%
III. Business Environment	8%
Total	100%

Domains, Tasks, and Enablers:

» Domain: Domain is defined as the high-level knowledge area that is essential to the practice of project management.
» Tasks: Tasks are the underlying responsibilities of the project manager within each domain area.
» Enablers: Illustrative examples of the work associated with the task. Please note that enablers are not meant to be an exhaustive list but instead offer a few examples to help demonstrate what the task encompasses.

Fundamental Concepts		
Project: Projects are defined as unique, temporary endeavors with a specific beginning and end. **Program**: A *program* is a group of related projects, subprograms, and program activities managed in a coordinated way to obtain benefits not available from managing them individually. **Project Management**: Project management is the application of knowledge, skills, tools, and techniques to complete project activities to meet project requirements. **Progressive elaboration**: involves continuously improving and detailing a plan as more detailed and specific information and more accurate estimates become available.	**Process**: 1 of 49 processes consisting *of inputs, tools & techniques* to produce specific *outputs* for the project **Project Life Cycle**: description determines the phases a project passes through from one inception to another. **Operations Management**: constitute an organization's ongoing, repetitive activities, such as accounting or production. **Project Phase**: is a collection of logically related project activities that culminates in the completion of one or more deliverables. **Baseline documents**: The original plan plus all approved changes to scope, schedule or cost.	**Project management business documents**: These are documents such as benefits management plan and business case created which captures data for the intent of the business. **Lessons Learned**: documented variances used to avoid variances in future projects **Portfolio**: refers to projects, programs, subportfolios, and operations managed as a group to achieve strategic objectives. **Project Data and Information**: These are the Work performance data, Work performance information, and Work performance reports documents created for the various stakeholder it is intended.

Project Roles

Project manager: The project manager has the responsibility of leading and managing the project throughout its entire life cycle.

Project coordinator: Maintaining and monitoring project plans, project schedules, work hours, budgets and expenditures.

Project expeditor: checks for problems, monitoring changes in the project, ensuring that the schedule is followed and tracking the status of all tasks to assure the the project deliverables will be ready on time and within budget.

Program Manager: directing all efforts of the projects and project managers.

Project sponsor: is primarily concerned with ensuring that the project delivers the agreed business benefits.

Senior management: is responsible for planning and directing the work of a group of individuals.

Stakeholder: have responsibilities to businesses that include educating developers, financing projects, creating scheduling parameters and setting milestone dates.

Functional Manager: manages and owns the resources in a specific department, such as IT, engineering, public relations, or marketing, and generally directs the technical work of individuals from that functional area who are working on the project.

Project Management Office: is a central place to make sure company standards, procedures and practices are being followed to ensure projects are successful.

Organization Types & Project Manager Power

Functional Matrix. This is the practice of managing individuals with more than one reporting line.

Weak Matrix. In this form of organization, the functional manager retains most of the power; they "own" the people and resources. In a weak/functional matrix, the project manager is not very powerful.

Balanced Matrix. A two-dimensional management structure (matrix) in which employees are assigned to two organizational groups: a functional group based on skill sets, which has a functional manager (vertical), and a specific project group, in which employees report to a product manager (horizontal).

Strong Matrix or **Project Matrix.** The project manager has most of the power, resources, and control over the work.

Diagram Of Matrix Organizational types

Process Frame Work

Process Groups (5)
Initiating processes
Planning processes
Executing processes
Monitoring and controlling processes
Closing processes
Knowledge Areas (10)
Integration Management
Scope Management
Schedule Management
Cost Management
Quality Management
Human resource Management
Communication Management
Risk Management
Procurement Management
Stakeholder Management

Common Inputs, Tools, and Outputs

Inputs: Organizational Process Assets (OPA), Enterprise Environmental Factors (EEF), Project Management Plan, Risk Register, Work Performance Data, Work Performance Reports

Tools: Expert Judgement, Meetings, Analytical Techniques, Facilitation Techniques, Project Management Information Systems (PMIS)

Outputs: Change Requests, Updates (Project Management Plan, Projects documents, and OPA) Work Performance Information

Integration Management Diagram

	Project Management Process Groups (49)				
Knowledge Areas	Initiating	Planning	Executing	Monitoring and Controlling	Closing
[4] Project Integration Management	4.1 Develop Project Charter	4.2 Develop Project Management Plan	4.3 Direct and Manage Project Work 4.4 Manage Project Knowledge	4.5 Monitor and Control Project Work 4.6 Perform Integrated Change Control	4.7 Close Project or Phase
[5] Project Scope Management		5.1 Plan Scope Management 5.2 Collect Requirements 5.3 Define Scope 5.4 Create WBS		5.5 Validate Scope 5.6 Control Scope	
[6] Project Schedule Management		6.1 Plan Schedule Management 6.2 Define Activities 6.3 Sequence Activities 6.4 Estimate Activity Durations 6.5 Develop Schedule		6.6 Control Schedule	
[7] Project Cost Management		7.1 Plan Cost Management 7.2 Estimate Costs 7.3 Determine Budget		7.4 Control Costs	
[8] Project Quality Management		8.1 Plan Quality Management	8.2 Manage Quality	8.3 Control Quality	
[9] Project Resource Management		9.1 Plan Resource Management 9.2 Estimate Activity Resources	9.3 Acquire Resources 9.4 Develop Team 9.5 Manage Team	9.6 Control Resources	
[10] Project Communications Management		10.1 Plan Communications Management	10.2 Manage Communications	10.3 Monitor Communications	

[11] Project Risk Management		11.1 Plan Risk Management 11.2 Identify Risks 11.3 Perform Qualitative Risk Analysis 11.4 Perform Quantitative Risk Analysis 11.5 Plan Risk Responses	11.6 Implement Risk Responses	11.7 Monitor Risks	
[12] Project Procurement Management		12.1 Plan Procurement Management	12.2 Conduct Procurements	12.3 Control Procurements	
[13] Project Stakeholder Management	13.1 Identify Stakeholders	13.2 Plan Stakeholder Engagement	13.3 Manage Stakeholder Engagement	13.4 Monitor Stakeholder Engagement	

Project Integration Management

Process	Inputs	Tools and Techniques	Outputs
4.1 Develop Project Charter	Business documents	Expert Judgments Data gathering Interpersonal skills Meetings	Project charter Assumptions log

Process	Inputs	Tools and Techniques	Outputs
4.2 Develop Project Management Plan	Project charter Outputs from other processes EEF	Expert Judgments Data gathering	Project management plan

Process	Inputs	Tools and Techniques	Outputs
4.3 Direct and Manage Project Work	Project management plan Project documents » Change log » Lessons learned register » Milestones list » Project communications » Project schedule » Requirements traceability matrix » Risk register » Risk report Approved change requests OPA EEF	Expert Judgments PMIS Meetings	Deliverables Work performance data Issues log Change requests PMP updates Project documents updates Activity list Assumptions log Lessons learned register Requirements documentation Risk register Stakeholder register OPA updates

Process	Inputs	Tools and Techniques	Outputs
4.4 Manage Project Knowledge	Project management plan Project documents » Lessons learned register » Project team assignments » Resource breakdown structure » Stakeholder register Deliverables OPA EEF	Expert Judgments Knowledge Management Information Management Interpersonal and team skills » Active listening » Facilitation » Leadership » Networking » Political awareness	Lessons learned register PMP updates OPA updates

Process	Inputs	Tools and Techniques	Outputs
13.4 Monitor Stakeholder Engagement	Project management plan » Scope management plan » Schedule management plan » Costs management plan » Quality management plan » Human resources management plan » Risks management plan » Communication management plan » Procurement management plan » Stakeholder management plan » Requirements management plan » Scope baseline » Schedule baseline » Cost baseline Project documents » Assumptions log » Basis of estimates » Cost forecasts » Issues log » Quality report » Lessons learned register » Milestone list » Risk register » Risk report » Schedule forecast Work performance information » Deliverables » Implementation status for change requests » Forecast estimates to complete EEF OPA	Data analysis » Alternative analysis » Cost-benefit analysis » Earned value analysis » Root cause analysis » Trend analysis » Variance analysis Estimate at completion Schedule forecasts Cost forecasts Decision-making Meetings	Work performance reports » Status reports » Progress reports » Change requests » Project management plan updates » Resource management plan » Communications management plan » Stakeholder engagement plan Project documents updates » Cost forecasts » Issues log » Lessons learned register » Project communications » Risk register » Stakeholder register » Schedule forecasts

Process	Inputs	Tools and Techniques	Outputs
4.6 Perform Integrated Change Control	Project management plan » Change management plan » Configuration management plan » Cost baseline » Schedule baseline » Scope baseline Project documents » Basis of estimates » Requirement traceability matrix » Risk report Work performance reports Change requests OPA EEF	Expert judgments Change control tools Data analysis » Alternative analysis » Cost-benefit analysis Decision-making » Voting » Autocratic decision-making » Multicriteria decision analysis Meetings	Approved change requests Project management plan updates Project documents updates

Process	Inputs	Tools and Techniques	Outputs
4.7 Close Project or Phase	Project charter Project management plan All components Project documents » Assumptions log » Basis of estimates » Change log » Issues log » Lessons learned register » Milestone list » Project communications » Quality control measurements » Quality report » Requirements documentation » Risk register » Risk report » Accepted deliverables » Business documents » Business case » Benefits management plan Agreements Procurement documents OPA	Expert judgments Data analysis » Document analysis » Regression analysis » Trend analysis » Variance analysis Meetings	Final product documents Final product, service, or result Final report OPA updates

Remarks about INTEGRATION MANAGEMENT

Business case describes why the project is necessary and includes information on funding the project.

Project selection methods offer a set of time-tested techniques based on sound logical reasoning to arrive at a choice of project and filter out undesirable projects with a very low likelihood of success.

Project Charter is a statement of the scope, objectives, and participants in a project. It provides a preliminary delineation of roles and responsibilities, outlines the project objectives, identifies the main stakeholders, and defines the authority of the project manager. It serves as a reference of authority for the future of the project.

Change requests may be necessary if you find that some activities were not initially discovered through progressive elaboration.

Closing process group is to conclude all activities across all project management process groups and formally complete the project, phase, or contractual obligations.

Project Scope Management

Process	Inputs	Tools and Techniques	Outputs
5.1 Plan Scope Management	Project charter Project management plan Quality management plan Project life cycle description Development approach EEF OPA	Expert judgments Data analysis » Alternative analysis for collecting requirements Meetings	Scope management plan Requirements management plan

Process	Inputs	Tools and Techniques	Outputs
5.2 Collect Requirements	Project charter Project management plan Project documents Business documents Agreements EEF OPA	Expert judgments Data gathering » Benchmarking Data analysis » Document analysis Decision-making » Voting » Multicriteria analysis Data representation » Affinity diagram » Mind mapping Interpersonal and team skills Context diagram Prototypes	Requirements documentation Requirements traceability matrix

Process	Inputs	Tools and Techniques	Outputs
5.3 Define Scope	Project charter Project management plan » Scope management plan Project documents EEF OPA	Expert judgments Data analysis » Alternative analysis Decision-making » Multicriteria decision analysis Interpersonal and team skills » Facilitation Product analysis	Project scope statement Project document updates

Process	Inputs	Tools and Techniques	Outputs
5.4 Create WBS	Project management plan » Scope management plan Project documents » Project scope statement » Requirements document EEF OPA	Expert judgments Decomposition	Scope baseline Project scope statement WBS Work package WBS dictionary Planning package Project document updates

Process	Inputs	Tools and Techniques	Outputs
5.5 Validate Scope	Project management plan » Scope management plan » Requirements management plan Project documents » Lessons learned register » Quality report » Requirements documentation » Requirements traceability matrix » Verified deliverables » Work performance data	Inspection Decision-making » Voting	Acceptable deliverables Work performance information Change requests Project documents updates » Lessons learned register » Requirements documentation » Requirements traceability matrix

Process	Inputs	Tools and Techniques	Outputs
5.6 Control Scope	Project management plan » Scope management plan » Requirements management plan » Change management plan » Configuration management plan » Scope baseline Performance measurement baseline Project documents » Lessons learned register » Requirements documentation » Requirements traceability matrix Work performance data OPA	Data analysis » Variance analysis » Trend analysis	Work performance information Change requests Project management plan updates » Scope management plan » Schedule baseline » Cost baseline » Scope baseline » Performance measurement baseline Project documents » Lessons learned register » Requirements documentation » Requirements traceability matrix

Remarks about SCOPE MANAGEMENT

Delphi technique is used to solicit information anonymously and gather honest feedback by eliminating intimidation.

Data analysis includes the stakeholder analysis of its interests, legal rights, ownership, knowledge, and contribution. It may also include analyzing documents from previous projects.

Data representation is an exercise in which the stakeholders are represented in a model such as a power/ interest grid, a power influence grid, or an impact/influence grid. (See the figure below.)

Alternative analysis is the evaluation of the different choices available to achieve a particular project management objective.

Variance analysis is used to compare the baseline to the actual results.

Trend analysis is used to determine if there is a pattern such as whether the performance is improving or deteriorating over time.

WBS Diagrams on the Exam

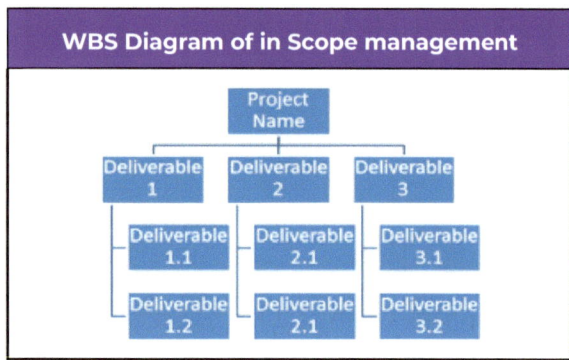

Project Schedule Management

Process	Inputs	Tools and Techniques	Outputs
6.1 Plan Schedule Management	Project charter Project management plan » Scope management plan Development approach EEF OPA	Expert judgments Data analysis » Alternative analysis » Rolling wave Meetings	Schedule management plan

Process	Inputs	Tools and Techniques	Outputs
6.2 Define Activities	Project management plan » Schedule management plan » Scope baseline EEF OPA	Expert judgments Decomposition Rolling wave planning Meetings	Activity list Activity attributes Milestone list Change requests PMP updates » Schedule baseline » Cost baseline

Process	Inputs	Tools and Techniques	Outputs
6.3 Sequence Activities	Project management plan » Schedule management plan » Scope baseline Project documents EEF OPA	Precedence diagramming method (PDM) Dependency determination and integration » Mandatory dependency » Discretionary dependency » External dependencies » Internal dependencies Leads and lags PMIS	Project schedule network diagram Project documents updates

Process	Inputs	Tools and Techniques	Outputs
6.4 Estimate Activity Durations	Project management plan Project documents » Activity attributes, activity list, assumption log » Lessons learned register » Milestone list » Project team assignments » Resource breakdown structure (RBS) » Resource calendars » Resource requirements » Risk register EEF OPA	Expert judgments Analogous estimating Parametric estimating Three point estimating Bottom-up estimating Data analysis » Alternative analysis » Reserve analysis Decision-making Meetings	Duration estimates Basis estimates Project documents updates Activity attributes Assumption log Lessons learned register

Process	Inputs	Tools and Techniques	Outputs
6.5 Develop Schedule	Project management plan » Schedule management plan » Scope baseline Project documents » Activity attributes, activity list, assumption log » Basis of estimates » Duration estimates » Lessons learned register » Milestone list » Project schedule network diagrams » Project team assignments » Resource breakdown structure (RBS) » Resource calendars » Resource requirements » Risk register » Agreements EEF OPA	Schedule network analysis » Critical path method » Resource optimization Data analysis » What-if scenario analysis » Monte Carlo simulation Leads and lags Schedule compression PMIS Agile release planning	Schedule baseline Project schedule » Schedule data » Project calendars » Change requests Project management plan updates » Schedule management plan » Cost baseline Project documents updates » Activity attributes, activity list, assumption log » Duration estimates » Lessons learned register » Resource requirements » Risk register

Process	Inputs	Tools and Techniques	Outputs
6.6 Control Schedule	Project management plan » Schedule management plan » Scope baseline » Schedule baseline » Performance measurement baseline Project documents » Lessons learned register » Project calendars » Project schedule » Resource calendars » Schedule data Work performance data OPA	Data analysis » Earned value analysis » Iteration burndown chart » Performance reviews » Trend analysis » Variance analysis » What-if scenario analysis Project management software Critical path method PMIS Resource optimization Leads and lags Schedule compression	Work performance information Schedule forecasts Change requests Project management plan updates » Schedule management plan » Schedule baseline » Performance measurement baseline Cost baseline » Project documents updates » Assumption log » Basis of estimates » Lessons learned register » Project schedule » Resource calendars » Schedule data

Remarks about SCHEDULE MANAGEMENT

Decomposition is the process of creating WBS work packages into activities.

Rolling wave planning is a technique wherein work to be completed in the near term is planned in detail, while work further in the future is planned at a higher level.

Milestone list is a list of significant points or events in a project.

critical path is the sequence of activities that represents the longest path through a project, which determines the shortest duration.

Resource optimization is used to adjust the start and finish dates of activities to match adjusted planned resource availability. Adjusting the schedule for resource optimization includes either resource leveling or resource smoothing.

Resource leveling is used when shared or critically required resources are only available at certain times or in limited quantities or are overallocated, such as when a resource has been assigned to two or more projects during the same time.

Resource smoothing does not change the critical path, and the completion date may not be delayed because with resource smoothing, the activities are adjusted on the schedule model so the requirements for resources on the project do not exceed certain predefined resource limits.

What-if scenario analysis is the process of changing the values in cells to see how those changes will affect the outcome of formulas on the worksheet.

Monte Carlo simulation is a quantitative risk-analysis technique used to identify the risk level of completing the project.

Schedule compression is used to shorten the schedule duration without reducing the project scope to meet imposed constraints.

Crashing shortens schedule duration by adding resources, such as approving overtime or paying to expedite delivery to activities on the critical path.

Fast-tracking is when activities normally done in sequence are performed in parallel for at least a portion of their duration.

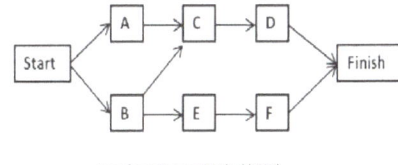

Precedence Diagram Method (PDM)

Analogous estimating is cost estimating based on a previous project similar to the current one.

Parametric estimating uses a similar previous project with a statistical relationship between historical data and variables.

Bottom-up estimating is the most accurate way to estimate costs because each work package in the WBS is analyzed.

Three-point estimating uses a formula based on most likely, optimistic, and pessimistic time estimates.

Reserve analysis estimates include contingency reserves. As more information becomes available through progressive elaboration, the contingency reserve is changed, reduced, and possibly eliminated.

Voting is used to select for best response involving project team members when discussing cost estimates.

Schedule forecasts are the computed time estimates of the earn value management (EVM) compared against schedule baseline.

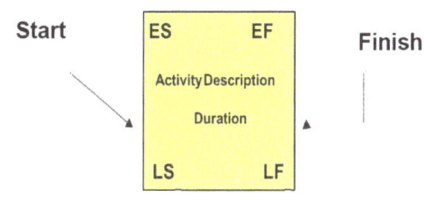

Project Cost Management

Process	Inputs	Tools and Techniques	Outputs
7.1 Plan Cost Management	Project charter Project management plan » Schedule management plan » Risk management plan EEF OPA	Expert judgments Data analysis » Alternative analysis Self-funding Funding with equity or debt Making resources Purchasing resources Renting resources Leasing resources Meetings	Cost management plan » Units of measure » Level of precision » Level of accuracy » Control threshold Strategic funding choices Procedures for fluctuations in currency Procedure for project cost recording

Process	Inputs	Tools and Techniques	Outputs
7.2 Estimate Costs	Project management plan » Cost management plan » Quality management plan » Scope baseline » Project scope statement » WBS » WBS dictionary Project documents » Lessons learned » Project schedules » Resource requirements » Risk register EEF OPA	Expert judgments Analogous estimating Parameter estimating Bottom up estimating Three point estimating Data analysis » Alternative analysis » Reserve analysis » Cost of quality PMIS Decision-making » voting	Cost estimates » Quantitative assessments » Contingency amounts » Basis of estimates Project documents updates » Lessons learned » Project schedule » Risk register

Process	Inputs	Tools and Techniques	Outputs
7.3 Determine Budget	Project management plan » Cost management plan » Resource management plan » Scope baseline Project documents » Basis estimates » Cost estimates » Project schedule » Risk register Business documents » Business case » Benefits management plan Agreement s EEF OPA	Expert judgments Cost aggregation Data analysis » Reserve analysis Historical information review » Analogous estimates » Parametric estimates Funding limitation reconciliation Financing	Cost baseline Project funding requirements Project documents updates » Cost estimates » Project schedule » Risk register

Process	Inputs	Tools and Techniques	Outputs
6.6 Control costs	Project management plan » Cost management plan » Cost baseline » Performance measurement baseline Project documents » Lessons learned register » Project funding requirements » Work performance data OPA	Expert judgments Data Analysis » Earned value analysis » Variance analysis » Trend analysis » What if scenario analysis » To-complete performance index (TCPI) PMIS	Work performance information Cost forecasts Change requests Project management plan updates » Cost management plan » Cost baseline » Performance measurement baseline Project documents updates » Assumption log » Basis of estimates » Cost estimates » Lessons learned register » Risk register

Remarks about COST MANAGEMENT

Cost forecasts are the computed cost estimates of the earn value management (EVM) compared against cost baseline.

Earned value analysis is used to capture information on schedule forecasts and cost forecasts.

Estimate at completion (EAC) is a forecast of the project's final cost.

Estimate to Completion (ETC) is how long until completion which is the EAC – AC.

Earn Value Management Formulas and Meanings		
Abbr.	Terminology	Formula
CV	Cost Variance	EV - AC
SV	Schedule Variance	EV - PV
CPI	Cost Performance Index	EV / AC
SPI	Schedule Performance Index	EV / PV
EAC	Estimate at Completion	AC + (BAC - EV)
		BAC / CPI
		AC + [(BAC-EV) / (CPI*SPI)]
ETC	Estimate to Completion	EAC - AC
VAC	Variance at Completion	BAC - EAC
TCPI	To Complete Performance Index	(BAC - EV) / (BAC - AC)
		(BAC - EV) / (EAC - AC)

To Complete Performance Index (TCPI) is the Cost performance needed to complete work Assumes original budget cannot be met which is BAC - EV) / (BAC - AC) or (BAC - EV) / (EAC - AC)

Variance at Completion (VAC) determine is forecast to be over or under budget for the project which is BAC-EAC.

Cost Performance Index (CPI) determine rate the project is spending money which is calculated with EV / AC=CPI

Schedule Performance Index (SPI) determines rate the project team is working which is calculate with EV / PV=SPI

Cost variance (CV) is defined as the "difference between earned value and actual costs. (CV = EV – AC)

Schedule variance (SV), which measures the difference between the earned value (EV) (the value of work actually performed) and the planned value (PV), so SV = EV – PV

Planned Value (PV) is the authorized budget assigned to work to be accomplished for an activity

Budget at Completion (BAC) refers to the sum of all **budget** values that have been previously established for the work to be performed on a project, or on components within a project

Cost baseline is used as an example in which cost performance is measured and monitored to gauge the importance of the project. This cost baseline is created by estimating the costs by the period in which the project would be completed.

Project Quality Management

Process	Inputs	Tools and Techniques	Outputs
8.1 Plan Quality Management	Project charter Project management plan » Requirements management plan » Risk management plan » Stakeholder engagement plan » Scope baseline Project documents » Assumptions log » Requirements documentation » Requirements traceability matrix » Risk register » Stakeholder register OPA EEF	Expert judgments Data gathering » Benchmarking » Brainstorming » Interviews Data analysis » Cost-benefit analysis » Cost of quality Data representation » Flowcharts » Logical model » Matrix diagrams » Mind mapping » Decision-making » Multicriteria analysis » Test and inspection Meetings	Quality management plan PMP updates » Risk management plan » Scope baseline Quality metrics Project documents updates » Lessons learned register » Requirements traceability matrix » Risk register » Stakeholder register

Process	Inputs	Tools and Techniques	Outputs
8.2 Manage Quality	Project management plan » Quality management plan Project documents » Lessons learned register » Quality control measurements » Quality metrics » Risk report OPA	Data gathering » Checklists Data analysis » Alternative analysis » Document analysis » Process analysis » Root cause analysis Decision-making » Multicriteria decision analysis Data representation » Affinity diagrams » Cause-and-effect diagrams » Flowcharts » Histograms » Matrix diagrams » Scatter diagrams Audits Design for X Problem-solving Quality improvement methods	Quality reports Test and evaluation documents Change requests PMP updates » Quality management plan » Scope baseline » Schedule baseline » Cost baseline » Project documents updates » Issues log » Lessons learned register » Risk register

Process	Inputs	Tools and Techniques	Outputs
8.3 Control Quality	Project management plan » Quality management plan » Project documents » Lessons learned register » Quality metrics » Test and evaluation documents » Approved change requests » Deliverables Work performance data OPA EEF	Data Gathering » Checklists » Check sheets/tally sheets » Statistical gathering » Questionnaires/surveys Data analysis » Performance reviews » Root cause analysis Inspection Testing/product evaluations Data representation » Cause-and-effect diagrams » Flowcharts » Check sheets » Pareto diagrams » Histograms » Control charts » Scatter diagrams Meetings	Quality control measurements Verified deliverables Work performance information Change requests Project Management plan updates » Quality management plan Project documents updates » Issues log » Lessons learned register » Risk register » Test and evaluation documents

Remarks about QUALITY MANAGEMENT

Cost of quality (COQ) refers to the total costs needed to bring products or services up to standards defined by project management professionals.

Inspection is when the contractor performs the structural review of the work—either a review of the deliverables or a physical review.

"Prevention over inspection" means that it costs less to prevent quality issues than it does to correct; meaning better control over your budgets.

One Sigma 68% of the observations in a process would be within one standard deviation

Two Sigma 95% of the observations in a process would be within two standard deviation

Three Sigma 99.73 of the observations in a process would be within three standard deviation

Six Sigma method focuses on understanding customers' requirements better and eliminating defects and waste. 3.4 defects per million; 99.99966% meet specifications

Quality control measurements are the documented results of control quality.

Seven Basic tools diagram in Quality management	Quality Management control tools
1. **Check sheets** are simple tally sheets that are used to gather data. Use this template when categorizing how often a problem occurs. 2. **Pareto diagram** is a chart that consists of a vertical bar and sometimes a bar-and-line graph. The vertical bar represents the frequency of defects from most to least, and the line represents a cumulative percentage of the defects. 3. **Histogram chart** is a bar graph that illustrates the frequency of an event occurring using the height of the bar as an indicator. 4. **Scatter diagrams** allow you to analyze the relationship between two variables. 5. **Control chart** is a graphic display of process data over time and against established control limits that has a centerline that assists in detecting a trend of plotted values toward either control limit. 6. **Cause-and-effect diagram, Fishbone, Ishakawa** is a tool that can help you perform a cause-and effect analysis for a problem you are trying to solve. This type of analysis enables you to discover the root cause of a problem. 7. **Flowcharts** above provide visual representations of project processes.	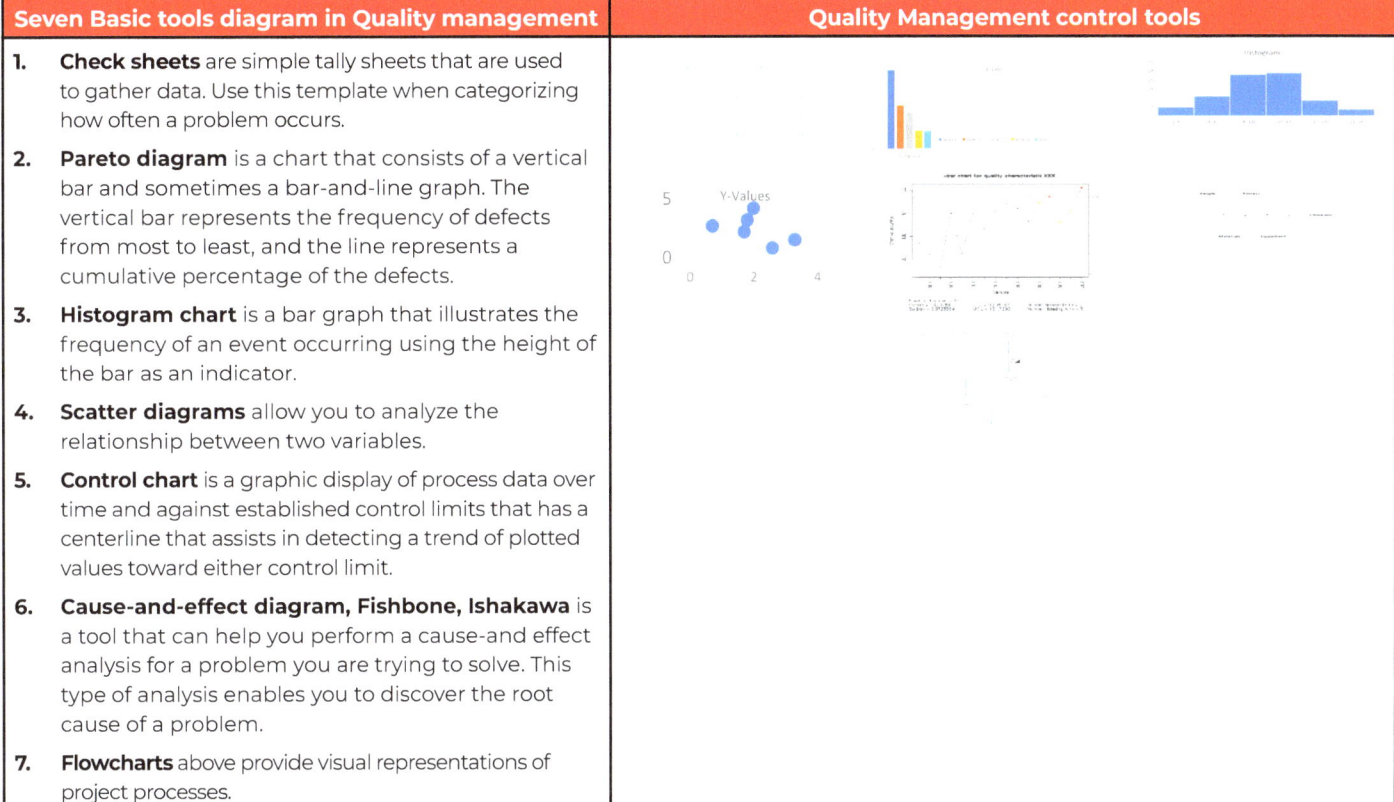

Project Human Resources Management

Process	Inputs	Tools and Techniques	Outputs
9.1 Plan Resource Management	Project charter Project management plan » Quality management plan » Scope baseline » Project documents » Project schedule » Requirements documentation Risk register Stakeholder register OPA EEF	Expert judgments Data representation » Hierarchical charts » Responsibility assignment matrix » Text-oriented formats » Organizational theory Meetings	Resource management plan Team charter PMP updates » Assumption log » Risk register

Process	Inputs	Tools and Techniques	Outputs
9.2 Estimate Activity Resources	Project management plan » Resource management plan » Scope baseline Project documents » Activity attributes » Activity list » Assumption log » Cost estimates » Resource calendars » Risk register OPA EEF	Expert judgments Analogous estimating Parametric estimating Three point estimating Bottom-up estimating Data analysis	Resource requirements Basis estimates Resource breakdown structure (RBS) Project document updates » Activity attributes » Assumption log » Lessons learned register

Process	Inputs	Tools and Techniques	Outputs
9.3 Acquire Resources	Project management plan » Resource management plan » Procurement management plan » Cost baseline Project documents » Project schedule » Resource calendars » Resource requirements » Stakeholder register OPA EEF	Decision-making » Multicriteria analysis Interpersonal skills » Negotiation Pre-assignment Virtual teams	Physical resource assignments Project team assignments Resource calendars Change requests PMP updates » Resource management plan » Cost baseline Project documents updates » Lessons learned register » Project schedule » RBS » Resource requirements » Risk register » Stakeholder register EEF updates OPA updates

Process	Inputs	Tools and Techniques	Outputs
9.4 Develop Team	Project management plan » Resource management plan Project documents » Lessons learned register » Project schedule » Project team assignments » Resource calendars » Team charter OPA EEF	Colocation Virtual teams Mixed locations Communication technology Interpersonal and team skills » Conflict management » Influencing » Motivation » Negotiation » Team building Recognition and rewards Training Individual and team assessments Meetings	Team performance assessments Change requests PMP updates » Resource management plan Project documents updates » Lessons learned register » Project schedule » Project team assignments » Resource calendars » Team charter » EEF updates » OPA updates

Process	Inputs	Tools and Techniques	Outputs
9.5 Manage Team	Project management plan » Resource management plan Project documents » Issues log » Lessons learned register » Project team assignments » Team charter Work performance report Team performance OPA EEF	Interpersonal and team skills » Conflict management » Decision-making » Emotional intelligence » Influencing » Leadership PMIS	Change requests PMP updates » Resource management plan » Cost baseline » Schedule baseline Project documents updates » Issues log » Lessons learned register » Project team assignments EEF updates

Process	Inputs	Tools and Techniques	Outputs
9.6 Control Resources	Project management plan » Resource management plan Project documents » Issues log » Lessons learned register » Physical resource assignments » Project schedule » Resource breakdown structure » Resource requirements » Risk register Work performance data Agreements OPA	Data Analysis » Alternative analysis » Cost-benefit analysis » Performance reviews » Trend analysis » Problem-solving Interpersonal and team skills » Negotiation » Influencing PMIS	Work performance information Change requests PMP updates » Resource management plan » Schedule baseline » Cost baseline Project documents updates » Assumption log » Issues log » Lessons learned register » Physical resource assignments » Resource breakdown structure » Risk register

Remarks about HUMAN RESOURCE MANAGEMENT

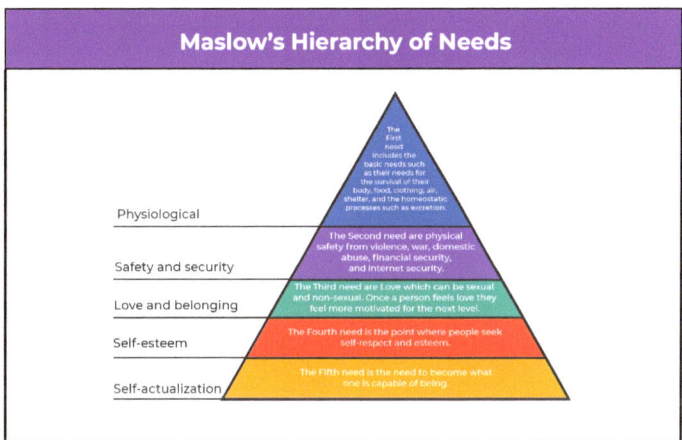

Herzberg's motivation-hygiene theory - states that there are certain factors in the workplace that cause job satisfaction while a separate set of factors cause dissatisfaction, all of which act independently of each other.

Project Communications Management

Process	Inputs	Tools and Techniques	Outputs
10.1 Plan Communications Management	Project charter Project management plan » Resource management plan » Stakeholder engagement plan Project documents » Requirements documentation » Stakeholder register OPA EEF	Expert judgments Communications requirements analysis Communication technology Communication models Communication skills PMIS Project reporting Interpersonal and team skills » Communication styles assessment » Political awareness » Cultural awareness Data Representation » Stakeholder engagement assessment matrix Meetings	Communications management plan PMP updates » Stakeholder engagement plan Project documents updates » Project schedule » Stakeholder register Organizational process assets updates

Process	Inputs	Tools and Techniques	Outputs
10.2 Manage Communications	Project management plan » Requirements management plan » Communications management plan » Stakeholder engagement plan Project documents » Change log » Issues log » Lessons learned register » Quality report » Risk report » Stakeholder register Work performance reports OPA EEF	Communications technology Communications methods Communications skills » Communications competence » Feedback » Nonverbal » Presentations PMIS Project reporting Interpersonal and team skills » Active listening » Conflict management » Cultural awareness » Meeting management » Networking » Political awareness Meetings	Project communications PMP updates » Communications management plan » Stakeholder engagement plan Project documents updates » Issues log » Lessons learned register » Project schedule » Risk register » Stakeholder register OPA updates

Process	Inputs	Tools and Techniques	Outputs
10.3 Monitor Communications	Project management plan » Resource management plan » Communications management plan » Stakeholder engagement plan Project documents » Issues log » Lessons learned register » Project communications Work performance data OPA EEF	Expert judgments PMIS Data analysis » Stakeholder engagement assessment matrix Interpersonal and team skills » Observation » Conversation skills Meetings	Work performance information Change requests Project management plan updates » Communications management plan » Stakeholder engagement plan Project document updates » Issues log » Lessons learned register

Remarks about COMMUNICATIONS MANAGEMENT

Communication channels is the number of communication channels be calculated using the formula N (N - 1) / 2; where N = the number of people.

Communication methods are interactive (multidirectional conversations), push (emails), and pull (shared storage, portals, or websites).

Communication models include encoding, which is transmitting the message, and decoding, which is receiving the message.

Communication technology includes shared portals, video and conferencing, chats, databases, social media, email, and websites.

Communications requirements analysis combines communications types and formats as needed to maximize the value of the information for project stakeholders.

Project Risk Management

Process	Inputs	Tools and Techniques	Outputs
11.1 Plan Risk Management	Project charter Project management plan » All subsidiary plans Project documents » Stakeholder register EEF OPA	Expert judgments Data analysis Meetings	Risk management plan » Methodology » Roles and responsibilities » Funding » Timing » Risk categories Probability and impact matrix Revised stakeholder tolerances Tracking

Process	Inputs	Tools and Techniques	Outputs
11.2 Identify Risks	Project management plan » Requirements management plan » Schedule management plan » Cost management plan » Quality management plan » Resource management plan » Risk management plan » Scope baseline » Schedule baseline » Cost baseline Project documents » Assumptions log » Cost estimates » Duration estimates » Issues log » Lessons learned register » Requirements documentation » Stakeholder register Agreements Procurement documents EEF OPA	Expert judgments Data gathering » Brainstorming » Checklists » Interviews Data analysis » Root cause analysis » Assumption and constraint analysis » SWOT analysis » Document analysis Interpersonal and team skills Facilitation Prompt lists Meetings	Risk register Risk report Project documents updates » Assumption log » Issues log » Lessons learned register

Process	Inputs	Tools and Techniques	Outputs
11.3 Perform Qualitative Risk Analysis	Project management plan » Risk management plan Project documents » Assumptions log » Risk register » Stakeholder register OPA EEF	Expert judgments Data gathering » Interviews of » Data analysts » Risk data quality assessment » Risk probability and impact assessment » Assessment of other risk parameters Interpersonal and team skills » Facilitation Risk categorization Data representation » Probability and impact matrix » Hierarchical charts	Project documents updates » Assumptions log » Issues log » Risk register » Risk report

Process	Inputs	Tools and Techniques	Outputs
11.4 Perform Quantitative Risk Analysis	Project management plan » Risk management plan » Scope baseline » Schedule baseline » Cost baseline Project documents » Assumption log » Basis of estimates » Cost estimates » Cost forecasts » Duration estimates » Milestone list » Risk register » Risk report » Schedule forecasts OPA EEF	Expert judgments Data gathering » Interviews Interpersonal and team skills » Facilitation Representations of uncertainty Data analysis » Simulations » Sensitivity analysis » Decision tree analysis » Influence diagrams	Project documents updates » Risk report » Assessment of overall project risks » Detail probabilistic analysis of project » Prioritized list of individual project risks » Trends in the quantitative risk analysis results » Recommended risk responses

Process	Inputs	Tools and Techniques	Outputs
11.5 Plan Risk Responses	Project management plan » Resource management plan » Risk management plan » Cost baseline Project documents » Lessons learned register » Project schedule » Project team assignments » Resource calendars » Risk register » Risk report » Stakeholder register OPA EEF	Expert judgments Data gathering » Interviews Interpersonal and team skills » Facilitation Data analysis » Alternative analysis Decision-making » Multicriteria decision analysis Contingency response strategies Strategies for overall project risk » Strategies for threats » Strategies for opportunities	Change requests Project management plan updates » Schedule management plan » Cost management plan » Quality management plan » Resource management plan » Procurement management plan » Scope baseline » Schedule baseline » Cost baseline Project documents updates » Assumptions log » Cost forecasts » Lessons learned register » Project schedule » Project team assignments » Risk register » Risk report

Process	Inputs	Tools and Techniques	Outputs
11.6 Implement Risk Response	Project management plan » Risk management plan Project documents » Lessons learned register » Risk register » Risk report OPA	Expert judgments Interpersonal skills Influencing PMIS	Change requests Project document updates » Issues log » Lessons learned register » Project team assignments » Risk register » Risk report

Process	Inputs	Tools and Techniques	Outputs
11.7 Monitor Risks	Project management plan » Risk management plan Project documents » Issues log » Lessons learned register » Risk register » Risk report Work performance data Work performance reports	Data analysis » Technical performance analysis » Reserve analysis Audits Meetings	Work performance information Change requests Project management updates Project documents updates » Assumptions log » Issues log » Lessons learned register » Risk register » Risk report OPA updates

Remarks about RISK MANAGEMENT

SWOT analysis analyzes the project's strengths, weaknesses, opportunities, and threats.
Risk categorization or grouping of risks is usually structured with a risk breakdown structure (RBS).
Probability impact matrix is the process of assessing the probabilities and consequences of risk events if they are realized.

Strategies for Threats	Strategies for Opportunities	Strategies for Project Risk	Contingent Response Strategies
» **Escalating** is appropriate when the threat is outside the scope of the project and at the program, portfolio, or another organizational level, but not at the project level. » **Avoidance** is when the project team acts to eliminate the threat or protect the project from its impact. In this case, the project team will attempt to remove the threat, extend the schedule, change the project schedule, or reduce the scope. » **Transference** involves shifting ownership to a third party, such as payment of insurance premiums so that if the risk occurs, its impact will be minimized. » **Mitigation** is action taken to reduce the probability the risk will occur, such as designing redundancy into the system that may reduce the impact of failure. » **Acceptance** acknowledges the existence of the threat. However, no action is taken.	» **Escalation** is appropriate when the opportunity is outside the scope of the project and at the program, portfolio, or other organizational levels, but not at the project level. » **Exploitation** is appropriate with high-priority opportunities where the organization wants to make sure the opportunity is realized, such as using a more talented resource to increase the chances that a task completes sooner. » **Sharing** involves transferring ownership to a third party. Examples of sharing actions include partnerships, teams, and joint ventures. » **Enhancement** is used to increase the probability or impact of an opportunity. Examples of enhancing opportunities are increasing resources such as fast-tracking and crashing to finish faster. » **Acceptance** acknowledges the existence of the opportunity. However, no action is taken.	» To avoid risk when a team member is not working out, that person must be released. Another cross-trained team member should take their place until a suitable replacement can be found. » **Exploit** high-priority opportunities where the organization wants to make sure the opportunity is realized, such as using a more talented resource to increase chances that a task completes sooner. » **Sharing** involves transferring ownership to a third party. Examples of sharing actions include partnerships, teams, and joint ventures. » **Acceptance** acknowledges the existence of the threat. However, no action is taken.	This type of response is only executed under predetermined conditions. When the risk does occur, there will be sufficient warning to implement the response plan, such as missing a milestone or a task gaining higher priority with the seller.

Project Procurement Management

Process	Inputs	Tools and Techniques	Outputs
12.1 Plan Procurement Management	Project Charter Business documents » Business case » Benefits management plan Project management plan » Scope management plan » Quality management plan » Resource management plan » Scope baseline Project documents » Milestone list » Project team assignments » Requirements document » Requirements traceability matrix » Resource requirements » Risk register » Stakeholder register OPA EEF	Expert judgments Data gathering Market research Data analysis » Make or buy analysis » Source selection analysis Meetings	Procurement management plan Procurement strategy Procurement statement of work Source selection criteria Make-or-buy analysis decision Independent cost estimates Change requests Project documents updates » Milestone list » Project team assignments » Requirements document » Requirements traceability matrix » Resource requirements » Risk register » Stakeholder register OPA updates Procurement documents Bid documents

Process	Inputs	Tools and Techniques	Outputs
12.2 Conduct Procurements	Procurement management plan » Scope management plan » Requirements management plan » Communications management plan » Risk management plan » Procurement management plan » Configuration management plan » Cost baseline Product documents » Lessons learned register » Project schedule » Requirements documentation » Risk register » Stakeholder register Procurement documents » Bid documents » Procurement statement of work » Independent cost estimates » Source selection criteria Seller proposals OPA EEF	Expert judgment Advertising Bidder conferences Data analysis » Proposal evaluation Interpersonal and team skills » Negotiation	Select sellers Agreements Change requests Project management plan updates » Requirements management plan » Quality management plan » Communications management plan Risk management plan » Procurement management plan » Cost baseline » Scope baseline » Schedule baseline Project documents updates » Lessons learned register » Requirements documentation » Requirements traceability matrix » Resource calendar » Risk register » Stakeholder register OPA updates

Process	Inputs	Tools and Techniques	Outputs
12.3 Control Procurements	Project management plan » Requirements management plan » Risk management plan » Procurement management plan » Change management plan » Schedule baseline Project documents » Assumptions log » Issues log » Lessons learned register » Milestone list » Quality report » Requirements documentation » Requirements traceability matrix » Risk register » Stakeholder register Agreements Procurement documentation Approved change requests Work performance data OPA EEF	Expert judgments Claims administration Data analysis » Performance reviews » Earned value analysis » Trend analysis Inspection Audits	Closed procurements Work performance information Procurement documentation updates Change requests Project management plan updates » Risk management plan » Procurement management plan » Schedule baseline » Cost baseline Project documents updates » Lessons learned register » Milestone list » Resource requirements » Requirements traceability matrix » Risk register » Stakeholder register OPA updates

Remarks about PROCUREMENT MANAGEMENT

Point of total assumption is the cost point in which the seller assumes 100% of the risk of additional cost increases.

PTA = ((Ceiling Price - Target Price)/buyer's Share Ratio) + Target Cost

Table of contract types, and risk			
Contract Types Versus Risk			
High ------------- Buyer's risk-------------------- Low			
CPPC	CPFF	CPIF	FPI
Cost plus percentage	Cost plus fixed fee	Cost plus incentive fee	Fixed price incentive
Low ------------- Seller's risk------------------- High			

Project Stakeholder Management

Process	Inputs	Tools and Techniques	Outputs
13.1 Identify Stakeholders	Project charter PMP » communications management plan » stakeholder engagement plan Business documents Project documents Agreements Enterprise environmental factors Organizational process assets	Expert judgments Data gathering Data analysis Data representation Meetings	Stakeholder register Change requests PMP updates Project documents updates

Process	Inputs	Tools and Techniques	Outputs
13.2 Plan Stakeholder Engagement	Project charter Project management plan Resource management plan Communications management plan Risk management plan » Projects documents » Assumptions log » Change log » Issue log » Project schedule » Risk register » Stakeholder register Agreement s OPA EEF	Expert judgments Data gathering » Benchmarking » Data analysis » Assumptions » Constraint analysis » Root cause analysis » Data representation » Prioritization/ ranking » Mind mapping » Stakeholder engagement matrix Meetings	Stakeholder engagement plan

Process	Inputs	Tools and Techniques	Outputs
13.3 Manage Stakeholder Engagement	Project Management Plan » Communications management plan » Risk management plan » Change management plan » Stakeholder engagement plan Project documents » Change log » Issues log » Lessons learned register » Stakeholder register OPA EEF	Expert judgments Communication skills » Feedback Interpersonal and team skills » Conflict management » Cultural awareness » Negotiation » Observation/ conversation » Political awareness » Ground rules Meetings	Change requests Project management plan updates » Communications management plan » Stakeholder engagement plan Project documents updates » Change log » Issues log » Lessons learned register » Stakeholder register OPA updates

Process	Inputs	Tools and Techniques	Outputs
13.4 Monitor Stakeholder Engagement	Project Management Plan » Resource Management Plan » Communications management plan » Stakeholder management plan Project documents » Change log » Issues log » Lessons learned register » Project communications » Stakeholder register Work Performance data OPA	Data analysis » Alternative analysis » Root cause analysis » Stakeholder analysis Decision making » Multicriteria decision analysis » Voting Data representation » Stakeholder engagement assessment matrix Communication skills » Feedback » Presentation Interpersonal and team skills » Active listening » Cultural awareness » Leadership » Networking » Political awareness Meetings	Work performance information Change requests Project management plan » Resource management plan » Communications management plan » Stakeholder engagement plan Project document updates » Issue log » Lessons learned register » Risk register » Stakeholder register

Remarks about STAKEHOLDER ENGAGEMENT MANAGEMENT

Stakeholder analysis grid(influence/interest) in Stakeholder management	
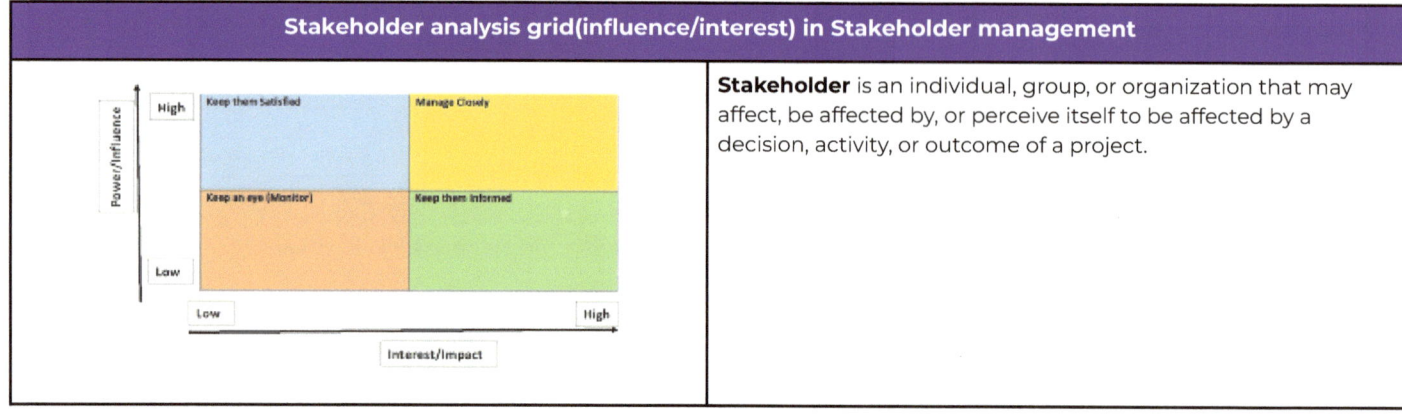	**Stakeholder** is an individual, group, or organization that may affect, be affected by, or perceive itself to be affected by a decision, activity, or outcome of a project.

Best Exam Tips

Six Tips for Passing the PMP Exam	
The most helpful thing I did was: Study hard and study smart. Study everything to smallest detail. *Leave nothing to chance.*	I read questions following where I was in the project management process *across left to right (initial, planning, execute, m/c or close) then down until I knew where the question was focusing in which process.*
Look for trends and patterns in the PMP material (such *as change requests are outputs in monitoring and control 9/10 times*).	I took the exam where I felt most comfortable and when I felt most comfortable. *(Bethesda, md: Sat 12:30pm)*
Take the mock exam until you pass with an 85% grade or greater consistently.	I had a good breakfast, a cup of coffee and a Monster drink, three hours before the exam. *Fuel and energy were not going to be an issue.*

PMBOK® is a registered trademark of Project Management Institute.

Project Management Professional (PMP)® is a registered trademark of Project Management Institute.

www.ingramcontent.com/pod-product-compliance
Lightning Source LLC
LaVergne TN
LVHW071031070426
835507LV00002B/116